The World God Made

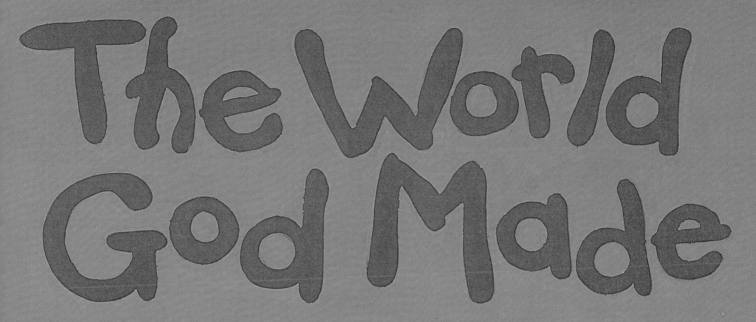

by Donna D. Cooner, Ed.D. illus. by Kim Simons

Tommy
NELSON

Thomas Nelson, Inc.
Nashville

To William and Anna who laid the foundation.
—DDC

For Chloe.
—KS

The World God Made
Copyright © 1994 by Donna Cooner for text.
Copyright © 1994 by Kim Simons for illustrations.
All rights reserved.
No portion of this book may be reproduced in any form without the written
permission from the publisher, except for brief excerpts in magazine reviews.

Managing Editor: Laura Minchew
Project Editor: Brenda Ward

Library of Congress Cataloging-in-Publication Data.

Cooner, Donna D. (Donna Danell)
 The world God made/by Donna Conner; illustrated by Kim Simons.
  p. cm.
  Summary: In the style of "The House That Jack Built," describes God's
creations, followed by a prayer of thanks.
  ISBN 0–8499–1162–1 (hardcover)
  ISBN 0–8499–5810–5 (tradepaper)
  [1. Creation—Fiction. 2. Nature—Fiction. 3. Stories in rhyme.]
 I. Simons, Kim, 1955– ill. II. Title.
PZ8.3.C779Wo 1994
[E]—dc20
                                                       94–3333
                                                         CIP
                                                         AC

Printed in the United States of America
97 98 99 00 01 LBM 9 8 7 6 5 4 3 2 1

This is the world
that God made.

This is the light
that shines on the world
that God made.

This is the sky
that's touched with the light
that shines on the world
that God made.

This is the field
that's under the sky
that's touched with the light
that shines on the world
that God made.

This is the stream
that runs through the field
that's under the sky
that's touched with the light
that shines on the world
that God made.

This is the tree
that grows by the stream
that runs through the field
that's under the sky
that's touched with the light
that shines on the world
that God made.

This is the cat
that climbs down the tree
that grows by the stream
that runs through the field
that's under the sky
that's touched with the light
that shines on the world
that God made.

This is the dog
that chases the cat
that climbs down the tree
that grows by the stream
that runs through the field
that's under the sky
that's touched with the light
that shines on the world
that God made.

This is the boy
that calls to the dog
that chases the cat
that climbs down the tree
that grows by the stream
that runs through the field
that's under the sky
that's touched with the light
that shines on the world
that God made.

Thank you, God, for the dog, quiet and good.
Thank you, God, for the cat, furry and small.

Thank you, God, for the tree, strong and tall.

Thank you, God, for the stream, cool and clear.

Thank you, God, for the field, grassy and near.

Thank you, God, for the sky, pink and gray.

Thank you, God, for the light's fading rays.

Thank you, God, for the world you made.

"God saw all that he had made, and it was very good."

Genesis 1:31